MW01641235

BECKONING HANDS FROM THE NEAR BEYOND

CONCRETE FACTS AND LAWS OF CONSCIOUS SPIRIT COMMUNION AND COMMUNICATION

BY

J. C. F. GRUMBINE

Author of
"Clairvoyance," "Telepathy," "Clairaudience," and numerous books on the
New Psychology

LONDON

L. N. FOWLER & Co

(C. R. King, Proprietor)

7 Imperial Arcade, Ludgate Circus, E.C.

1917

Printed by the Southampton Times Company, Limited
7[illegible] Above Bar, Southampton.

Reprinted
By
Health Research
P. O. Box 850
Pomeroy, Wa 99347
www.healthresearchbooks.com

FOREWORD

ARE we alive and immortal, or mere machines, wound up for a number of years, to run down and at last to be consigned to the scrap-heap called the grave? Or are we eternal and here on earth for the fleeting moment, to do our work, learn the needed lessons, serve and minister to others, and then pass on to higher spheres of spiritual life and unfoldment? Are the brief but happy relationships and companionships of mortals but the mere contiguity of an ocean vessel at a dock, with glad welcomes or good-byes and then the night-time of a never-broken absence and no returns? Are the human flowers like those of the field, which bloom in the summer, but perish in the winter, a rich blessing while they last, a painful memory when they are gone? If this is so, why, then, this struggle for existence, this tenacity for life, this obsession of domestic ties and kindred affections, this grip on outward possessions—wealth, name, fame, power, pleasure—if all is of a stage set for a play on which the curtain falls for ever when death closes one's eyes?

The reader, in his easy chair, has watched the birds flit by his window, or has seen the snow melt in the warm atmosphere, and suddenly on the street his eye has caught a funeral *cortège* passing up the hill to yonder cemetery. A moment later, but this time in reverie, he saw distinct visions of lovely, white-robed beings which lingered long enough to make him feel, if not know, there are no dead—and the funeral procession and the reverie were gone! Were you dreaming, my reader, when these visions appeared, or were they the living that you saw, who had laid aside the dead to be more alive, more conscious, and for ever in your presence? If you were a scientist, you would wish that that vision were photographed, so that, after brushing your eyes, you might believe that you did not imagine it, or were not deceived, and that you might have tangible evidence of a spiritual reality to give to the world. But this wish is one which all seers, all idealists, all lovers of visions who know that the spiritual is the real world, have wished since the night, and before that night, Jacob saw angels descending and ascending on a ladder of light. Beckoning hands from the near beyond have called and called to their brethren through the thin atmosphere; but the hands have been seen only by the few, whose testimony of so marvellous a vision has usually been discredited by the scientific photographers, whose eyes can see only the physical appearance of spirit, and who, in most cases, deny what cannot be impressed upon the retina of the physical eye or the sensitized photographer's plate. Still the hands are beckoning, and the wonder is that more eyes do not see them.

It is the purpose of this book to give technical knowledge which will aid the pilgrim to commune with his invisible helpers, and the sorrowful to feel the touch and see the vanished hand and hear the sound of a voice that is still. The path leading through these supernormal mysteries to this knowledge is not one of pleasure, nor one of pain, but of discipline, self-denial, abstemiousness, and purity. These conditions are demanded if results are expected, precisely as chemical results require obedience to chemical laws of combination. Still, the joy of the obtainment is in the labour of the attainment. No step toward the light, however it may seem to lead through the blind alleys of darkness, is without interest. The darkness is only in the appearance, for fuller consciousness is light thrown on each step—is, in fact, a disillusionment of mystery and dissolvent of darkness. If the student who believes in immortality or in the resurrection, or who is agnostic of the survival of the personality of death, will but apply conditions which supernormal psychology offer as a means to the end, evidences of spirit communion and communication will be realized.

CONTENTS

CHAPTER I

A Radical and Rational Change in our Conceptions of the Hereafter

Since the dawn of the New Christianity, the New Psychology, New and Higher Thought, Theosophy, and Spiritualism, views of the hereafter have radically changed. The rationalistic swing of the pendulum toward denial and agnosticism of a future life has passed to a scientific acceptance of the psychical facts as demonstrating not only the survival of the personality of death, but the evidential proof of spirit communion and communication. This astounding knowledge, equalled nor surpassed by no discovery of physical science, will mean more for the reconstruction of social and educational ideals and the renaissance of a spiritual civilization than all efforts growing out of the present System. Once death was the terror of man, and the grave the end or the beginning of misery. Now death, as a rule, is but a natural change from old, tired, or painful bodies and minds into young, strong, happy states of human development. No soul is worse off because of death. It does not widen, but rather narrows the breach between one's true self and one's life-work and destiny; for when the darkness which obstructs the ordinary mind is dispelled by death, a clearer perception of life, its purpose and its tremendous reality, are had. In the last fifty years decided changes have taken place as to human destiny. The theological as well as material conceptions of this life in relation to immortality have been discarded. The fact of the resurrection is a natural and not a supernatural change and event in the life of the soul. No longer does the Christian scoff at demonstrable evidences of the soul's immortality as possible outside of the Bible, but accepts Paul's conclusion as sound philosophy, established upon scientific proof, "that if there be no immortality of the dead, then is Christ (the Divine in us) not risen." The rejection of the supernatural and theological conception of the resurrection was not accomplished except by fierce and formidable opposition on the part of the Church, as though proof of a universal and indigenous immortality of the soul is, in the very nature of the fact, a death-blow to a true theological conception. A theological conception of immortality must agree with scientifically demonstrable facts; and when it fails to do so, its false and erroneous premise and conclusion destroy themselves. So has it been with the specious doctrine of the resurrection.

The theory that the soul sleeps with the body when it is interred has been exploded by modern Spiritualism; and yet, though the so-called dead do not sleep—for Christian theologians and dogmatists, following Egyptian traditions, taught that they did—the fear or sentiment that they do keeps the Christian Church from endorsing cremation as the sanest and most sanitary form of sepulture, while their burying-grounds or cemeteries in all large cities become evidences of how tenaciously land tenure as a legal restraint of civilization and enlightenment holds each grave inviolate until the judgment-day. Such leases of graves are made on theological as well as legal grounds, and their contracts end only with doomsday.

The new and electrical hypothesis of matter, that the atom is after all but a point of electrical energy, in which one thousand electrons play, is forcing home to mind the volatile and fluidic nature of matter. Once it stood as an eternal parallel of life, and a fixed substance. Now it has nterst ces, by which its solid form vanishes like a ghost into space or seeming nothingness, called ether. And this transformation or translation is going on all the time. There is no matter that is not in this state of flux. The soul is essentially permanent, at least, so far as comparisons with material forms extend; for while its expression proves and manifests change only from within without altering the soul itself, matter shows changes from without which alter its substances as well as its form. The entire physical universe is thus likened to the body through which the spirit operates. This hypothesis furnishes ground upon which Sir Oliver Lodge and Sir William Crookes build their ultra theories of an energy which, call it spirit or mind, is at the centre of everything, and is the indestructible entity which change may reveal but cannot destroy. Matter, therefore, instead of destroying all hopes of immortality, is now proving to be the veiled prophet of spirit, manifesting it as its latency and potentiality, concealed by its outward mask, but revealed when that mask is thrown aside.

Mind, too, has risen to a degree of vision not hitherto believed possible. It was once likened to the perfume of the flower, although

Plato, following his teacher Socrates. adjudged it a prisoner in a cell or a bird in a cage. Now science teaches that the perfume has not derived its fragrance from the body, but from the spirit, and lends the body its sweetness, as a vase receives the subtile emanations of a rose. For the mind is a substance that exists apart from the body, as is proven by telepathic and all supernormal phenomena, and, while it can be obsessed by the body, is yet free to follow inspirations, visions, ecstasies, voices, and its own Divinity. These mystical experiences have offered, and are offering, to and within the mind its highest and best credentials of its spiritual being! It is not now so much a question as to what matter is as to the law of its lmitations, for mind as psychical facts show, is not matter at all, and therefore is not subject to its limitations. More and more is consciousness forcing its spiritual origin rather than its physica manifestation upon man, and the far or near cry of the soul is for a square deal so far as the facts of consciousness are concerned.

It is deplorable, both for our loved ones on the spirit side of life and ourselves, that every noble effort to rationalize and bring within the sphere of natural law and human understanding the facts of spirit communication should be met so often by ridicule and sarcastic criticism from the Press and cold indifference from the Church, while the people clamour for each fresh fact or revelation from the Beyond.

Let the student of the spirit remember that " truth wears no mask, bows at no human shrine, seeks neither place nor applause: she only asks a hearing." And with this high purpose of truth definitely fixed in his mind, let him do his duty toward human freedom. Ignorance is the curse of the world; truth its liberator. Let the Church and the Press rather champion the truth, even at a sacrifice of their power and commercial success, than be guilty of insincerity and hypocrisy.

To-day, as always, the supreme question is not what I believe, but what I know of immortality. And this knowledge is more valuable and more to be sought for than any other possession, because it is fundamental to true education, vocational service, and happiness. Now that such knowledge is available no one need fear the future. Recent facts touching the soul's life after death prove that the old theological doctrine of salvation through atonement, and of rewards and punishment, is false. Life is governed by only one law, and that is the law of cause and effect. Whatsoever a man sows, that he reaps not only day by day, in his character, his conscience, his face, his life, but so long as he allows his thoughts and deeds to grip him in the clutches of this retributive law. There is no punishment nor reward in the law—only justice, and a justice so tempered with mercy that the effect lasts no longer than the cause. Justice is not to be measured by pleasure or pain, but it is a principle which demands righteousness, love, benevolence, truth, goodness of each one. Anatomic, physiological, and organic results follow an infringement of this law. The spirit people reveal to us that this law, known by the ancient teachers of India as karma, is expiatory only as error demands correction. Thus alone can the balance of life be maintained. It is neither natural nor true to imagine that the debts we owe the law will or can be paid in our present existence. This conclusion is not only sustained by the wisest and most just ethical teachers, but by the seers of all ages. The facts of spirit life also prove the conclusion. The doctrine of eternal punishment is not involved in this conclusion.

All evil and error cease at length under the law of human development. Error and evil are remedial, not punitive. They work as acids, burn as fires, but never destroy what they transform and glorify. A system of theology which teaches a future punishment for sin, obsolete as it is in pulpit and pew, ignoring the law of cause and effect, proves that it is grounded on error, and should be discarded. Yet the fear of death and terror of the grave have been emphasized by such false teachings. One of the purposes and needs of the present revelation concerning the life and fate of spirit people is to arouse in mankind a sincere respect for the science and knowledge of this life, its laws and facts, and to enforce such respect by proving that, though each earthly experience, however criminal, is tolerated and inevitable, yet the result of such action is not withdrawn nor cancelled by nature because of ignorance or disobedience. More than this, it shows that though pain may end on the physical plane because of death, *sorrow* for the thought or action may continue after death. But such sorrow is never punitive, as theology taught.

Again, while there is a lack of veneration among the young for old age and reverence for antiquity, while there is a passing of that form of idolatry and fetishism which canonized saints and sanctified books and relics, still it is doubtful if the extremity of levity which followed is justifiable in view of the deeper and stronger evidences now had of spiritual realities. The swing of the human mind and heart from religion to science does not justify immorality, agnosticism, nor a reckless disregard of and contempt for rational, moral, and spiritual ideals and standards of education and culture. If there is any meaning to a demonstrable scientific resurrection, a spiritual existence after death, and of the survival of the personal identity, it is the deeper and wider treatment of the daily facts and experiences of human life and character in the destiny of the soul. One round of the ladder betrays the upward, not parallel, progress of the spirit, and a broken round is neither secure for the so-called dead in their descent or for the living in their ascent of life. Error is never a foundation for spiritual consciousness, however it may serve as a spur to truth. It scars the flesh and mars the white cleanness of one's spiritual habiliments. Memory proves this, and it is an old saying that "past sins cast long shadows."

There is every reason for believing that we are in the midst of the new era of reconstruction. The iconoclastic age has done its work, and is slowly passing away. What man thinks is squaring itself with what man is. Service is the word which must dignify action, prove the divinity of the "golden rule" and the value we place upon our destinies. The polemic and militant must give place to the righteous and the divine. Selfishness must yield to co-operation in the most impersonal sense. A government of, for, and by the people must supplant a mere political form of rule in which might makes right, or in which a warfare is possible between capital and labour, autocratic minorities and democratic majorities. Education must have to do with one's vocation as determined by one's destiny and not by income or pleasure. Life, radiant, happy life, in which death will be but another opportunity for unfoldment, will then lay aside the visage of grim terror, worry, poverty, disease, and age, and shine with the light and the glory of eternity—as beautiful at sunrise as at sunsetting—a perpetual benediction.

CHAPTER II

Our Places and Occupations in the Spirit World

That the disembodied spirit has an occupation as vocational as any which engaged its attention when in a body on earth is one of the important revelations of modern Spiritualism. The Christian Church led its converts to believe that human occupations and destinies ended at death. Now Spiritualism proves by its general and universal evidence that our life on earth is but a phase of the soul's development, and a basic, progressive, rather than a final finishing step in its apotheosis. Souls are not loafing in the spirit world. The Buddhistic and esoteric Christian conception of work, the office and necessity of work, is in the Western world transplanting the theological. One's work is involved in one's life, as one's character is exalted or degraded by one's attitude to one's work. This is a reasonable and natural conception. It commends itself to common sense. It is shorn of romance and fiction. The facts of daily life hint at a plan which, however hidden, has its sidelights upon destiny and its revelations of eternity. It is rather strange that the human, natural, and rational development of both one's vocational work and character should be treated so inhumanly, unnaturally, and irrationally when dealing with our post-mortal life The anomaly of it strikes the most casual observer of life's experiences as extraordinary. Why, when dealing with religion and religious subjects, people should discard their reason and blindly, ignorantly, and credulously believe the impossible is one of the mysteries of the mind not intelligible to a thinker. Such blind and idiotic faith is not used when dealing with lands and houses, gold and silver, or material in any form. The concrete invites exact observation and demands rational acceptance. The abstract allows a wide field to speculation and imagination. When once, however, the spirit life is approached as a concrete substance, and not as though made of such stuff as dreams, then man will soberly weigh evidence, discard fiction, and deal with the spiritual realities from the standpoint of *facts*, and not theories or doctrines. This is what modern science demands. And who will deny that the scientific treatment of facts is not more profitable in the negative removal and destruction of error, and the positive perception and understanding of truth even, if the word "supernaturalism" is discarded, with the obsolete symbolisms and false doctrines established on the alleged miracles of Jesus Christ? Facts demand our acceptance. As a direct result of the scientific investigations of psychical phenomena, both abnormal and supernormal, it has been proven that the spirit world exists, and that we can have no longer any doubt of the "geography" of the spirit world, and that its substance is ether matter, as the substance of the material world is physical matter. Sir Oliver Lodge makes bold to announce his positive knowledge of this fact, and he goes so far as to say, both in his books and his addresses, that the ethereal substance which constitutes (to him) the matter of the spirit world is denser than matter in its present form—is, in fact, the essence of matter, as matter is known. And so it is neither fanciful nor unscientific to affirm that the geography and topography of the spirit world are as solid and various as the earth. Though incomprehensible to us, it would not be so if the spiritual as well as the ethereal world could be approached from solid to gaseous, coarse to fine, realizing by the law of correspondence that each sublimation of existence presupposes an adaptation as nice and natural as the relation of the eye to the light. The heavier-than-air machine, fanning the air at the height of eight thousand feet, was once thought impossible, yet motion generated by a gasoline machine solved the problem. The spirit, endowed with will, the greatest generator of motion in the universe, can and does move the physical body, yet on its own ethereal plane can project the spiritual body instantaneously where it wills and according to its attractions. And the sublimer the body and the purer the mind, the finer will be the spirit's attractions and environments, and, as a result, its exaltations and levitations. For this reason there is a gross and fine body, one the physical and the other the ethereal; and it is not unnatural nor strange that the coarser grades of matter should circumstance the one, while the finer grades should circumstance the other. In fact, such is the case, that in the spirit world the spirit whose body is physically gross, because of an earthly attraction, finds its counterpart, the ethereal body, darkened or beclouded in a smokelike aura, and this aura is an emanation of a spiritual condition which holds the spirit earth-bound. The Theosophists call this "karma," and consign the spirit thus afflicted to *kama loca* (the place of desire). This place of desire, so called, is none other than the grosser envelope of the spirit world, meteorologically and topographically speaking, which connects physical with ethereal matter. This may have been the place or state called by Dante and Milton "sheol" or hell, because of the varieties of lurid reds, dark browns, ugly purples, and menacing greens which emanate as auric atmospheres from the gross numbers of spirits who temporarily abide here. If it be true that there are seven distinct spheres in the spirit world, however graded each spirit or group of spirits may be in each sphere—spheres which in a mystical but not literal sense can be likened to the seven colours and notes—these spheres touch on the lower declination through the vibration of red, the negative, black, and on the upper inclination through the vibration of blue, the positive white light. And the reader will at once reflect and doubtless surmise the locality of the dark and white angels, one known as daemon (a force for evil) and the other diva (a god), each spirit having once been human and an inhabitant on earth; the intermediary intelligences varying in their development toward the light—that is, the Divinity potential or latent in each one, and which is susceptible of expression. That these spheres correspond to places as real as the ground we walk on and the houses in which we live, let the reader have no doubt, for if he can penetrate the connection between the spider and its web he will at once perceive how states of mind are interrelated with ethereal places or planes of inhabitation. As a man thinketh, so he spins his web in which he lives, daily spinning webs, for ever spinning webs, finer and brighter, unto the end!

Our occupations on the spirit side of life follow a natural bent and vocational adaptation. For instance, there are other ways of using the voice besides singing and speaking. In the spirit world great singers and orators are often inspirers, breathing upon the youth who are on earth and who are susceptible to their influence the inspiration to make the most of themselves in the wider and deeper meaning of culture, while at the same time they are unfolding themselves in the still deeper harmonies of the spiritual universe. For music is only one form of the expression of harmony. Again, Jesus and Buddha, one a carpenter's son and the other a prince, each pursued a vocation quite out of the natural order and yet spiritually related to their parents' hereditary pursuits. One turned away from the building of material houses, necessary as such construction work was, to the building of character—" the house not made with hands, eternal in the heavens "—while the other sought neither luxury nor ease in the palace of his father, the king, but became an outcast and mendicant, the better to liberate his people from the bondage of the senses and show them the way to Nirvana—peace. On the earth such were Messiahs, and in the higher life they still shine as suns, dispensing light to all who seek it. The distance between the spiritually undeveloped and the Christ or Budhha is in the saying, " I have overcome the world." Hence their oneness with God and the sense of separateness which others who are not so developed feel.

In our occupations on earth, whatever may be our speciality, there is involved a spiritual counterpart. An architect would be busy helping the unimaginative and unidealistic to attain to the beautiful, and so showing the souls who lived in and preferred squalor and ugly surroundings the connection between the law of beautiful living, our bodies, and the homes in which we live. The geographer would be connecting the contour and map of the earth with the ethereal planes which correspond with the physical surface, learning and showing the deeper spiritual relationship between them. The botanist would see and study the flowers just as on earth, but in their ethereality, radiant in outline and luminous in the colours which they emanate. The physicist and chemist will pursue their finer studies in the investigations and discoveries of the elements, laws, and forces which will mark the dawn of conscious knowledge of the oneness and unity of life, and they will forward to earth's inhabitants the results of their findings. So the inventor will never cease to plan, construct, and create what will work for greater human service, both in the spiritual spheres and on earth. Those who were irresponsible will be taught and learn responsibility. Those who seemed and were conscienceless will be made to obey the still small voice of the soul. Those who murdered will be taught to respect life, even that of a grovelling worm ; while those who were vain, proud, flippant, indifferent to life's highest uses and purposes, will come to learn how great is true worth, how dignified is labour, how sacred is one's honour and character, and how beneficial are all experiences of life. The falsifier will learn to so love truth that any sacrifice will not be too great to make for it. And on the spirit side of life such occupations as develop these phases of character will be chosen, in order to end the sorrow and dispel the shadow which errors made possible on the way from earth to heaven. When it is said that love, not hate: knowledge, not ignorance; truth, not error or falsehood; justice and mercy, and not force and cruelty, bring the most exalted stations in the spirit world, it implies that these virtues and their opposites have the same values on earth, although the results are not so evident. A person may be rich, and yet false, unjust, cruel, hateful, and ignorant. Such riches represent only temporal power, and abject weakness, humiliation, and misery after death until the soul expiates for his selfishness. And no doubt the occupation of any miser, like Scrooge in Dickens' *Christmas Carol,* will be to practise benevolence in whatever he does, in order to undo his past and improve his present spiritual station. So our occupations and vocations on the spirit side of life have the least to do with wages or what we can obtain in an objective sense, but what we can be or attain in a subjective or spiritual sense. Let the reader not flatter himself that the soul can divorce itself from its business on earth by the change called death. No such miracle is possible. Whatever magic death performs, it brings the soul the full harvest of whatever it has sown, good or evil, as the case may be. Nature never parries nor parleys. She does not temporize nor compromise. She pays her debts, and exacts the same obligation from all. As touching our occupations in the hereafter in the light of necessity, duty, and choice, the object and end of all labour is *soul unfoldment*, and not merely happiness. Happiness, joy, peace, are by-products or effects of such unfoldment. As the realization of truth is the object of art, and not "art for art's sake," so character is the measure of our love of both art and truth. The love of the beautiful as a sentiment, and which inspires the poet, artist, sculptor, and the individual in every walk of life, exists not to find its highest, purest expression merely in outward forms, but in character. And the soul that permits beauty to fashion its handiwork, or body, or dress, and not its life, is like an instrument which passively permits the musician to use it, but is only the instrument and nothing more. So a life is empty of spiritual values if its assets are merely "experiences" which have not impressed or influenced the soul with the solemn and urgent call of its Divinity. A wasted life on earth corresponds symbolically with an empty house, a desert of ice or sand, an abandoned farm, an extinct volcano, a dry well, a forsaken shell; and on the spirit side that symbol is fraught with deep meaning. The law of dissimilitude which operates on the spiritual side of our natures is only faintly perceived in its far-reaching inclusiveness. How often the remark is made, "You needed the experience, or you never would have had it"! Literally translated, the remark might apply to a trusted employé in a bank, office, or store who embezzles his employer's money. How incongruous to associate such a deed with such a man! A tramp, a thug, a highwayman, a criminal, or an outcast might be expected to commit such a deed, but these men, never. And yet, incongruous as the reputation of these trusted men is with their deed or character, the horrible experience proves that the character of the man becomes the judge of his reputation. Of course, one wrong act should not ruin the man, nor negative all the good he ever did; still, it proves the old saying that "All is not gold that glitters"; also, that one flaw in a steel rail may wreck a train. Some silly, foolish, or criminal deed may be tossed into the scale of life and outweigh a lifetime of "excellent" character; but nature, just in all her judgments, has no systems of rewards or punishments by which she balances her accounts, or by which she reaches and teaches a guilty soul.

Much so-called crime is such only in form and before man-made laws. Were we aware of the circumstances, contingencies, crises, and obsessions which led up to the crime, we might say "Not guilty" as we soberly consider the evidence. The world may blame, because the world is ignorant; but nature and conscience, yes, the spirit world, pardon such, and, to use the words of Jesus, add, "Neither do I condemn thee." But this mercy which tempers justice cannot make wrong right or right wrong. Before God our acts make or unmake us, and so a soul thus overshadowed is given a destiny, in which tests of character are offered in order to prove, not to tempt, the soul; and as iron is made steel by treatment, so experience, however dreadful, should calcine from the soul that which is no part of its Divinity. On the spirit side of life the soul shines in brightness because of its discipline, just as a diamond is radiant with colour through the skill of the lapidary who knows how to bring out the translucent glory of its innate beauty. The spirit world is not so unnatural as people have been led to imagine; for they have been led to believe that the Revelations of John are literal truth or visions of facts, instead of symbols which need a mystical key to interpret.

Finally, it would be foolish for us to believe that centrifugal and centripetal forces, further expressed as attraction and repulsion, hold the ponderous planets in their places, and yet deny the substantiality of the spirit world in which our loved ones live. The latest findings of physical science prove that the physical universe, solid and substantial as it seems, is in a condition of flux, at the centre of which is radiant matter so fine that a new word, "electrons" (not atoms), had to be coined to express the rarity and sublimity of its forms. And yet our solid, granitic rocks on which our houses are built rest on such a foundation. Is it, therefore, unscientific to expound the findings of science and say that this ethereality which is the solid base of the physical side of the universe is yet the base of the spiritual, and as a pyramid is to us on this plane of consciousness real in stone, it is none the less real as reflected in the Nile? Who will deny which world is the more enduring—the physical, which is the real, and the reflection, or the spiritual, which is the divine and eternal? So the law of dissimilitude shows us that the physical side of our life is but the reflection of the spiritual, and our places and occupations are correspondential.

CHAPTER III

Nature has Endowed Us with Faculties to Communicate with the Departed

Is there a more pathetic spectacle than the parlour of a home in which the dead body of a loved one—it may be the mother or father, the wife or husband, or the child—rests in its coffin, while the mourners stand dumb before the mystery of death, powerless to penetrate the veil, to see, hear, or feel the spirit presence, and not know that the one who vacated the body is in their midst, unrecognized in the new condition? Yet this is a daily tragedy. If it be true that as many die as are born, then there is a reason why this earth is called a "sorrowing planet." The mourner, despite the hope and promise of institutional Christianity of a physical resurrection in the last days, derives scant comfort from the liturgy of the Church and the "I am the resurrection and the life," as pronounced by the clergy. Theology breaks down at the grave, and the rebellious

Christian rails at God, the Church, and the universe for the seemingly empty words and hollow promises of the chosen vicars of Christ. "Where are my dead?" they cry, in unconsolable bereavement, weeping as did Rachel, and refusing to be comforted. "Where, indeed?" the lonely soul may ask of ecclesiastical authority, who repeat at the grave as the dead are lowered into their last resting-place, "Dust to dust, ashes to ashes, earth to earth." The sunny or rainy sky reveal them not! The home is vacant without them, and their forms no longer stir the air or resound with their footsteps or their voices. The streets hold everyone but them. They are gone for ever from the places which knew them, and a stillness and heartache most bitter follow, which time only can lift. Where are they?

The very mourning which Fashion decrees that the bereaved should wear is a mockery and a shadow of darkness over them. It is so atheistic and infidel, so un-Christlike and unreasonable, as to for ever condemn it and institutional religion for tolerating it. And why? Because black is hopeless and a negative, symbolizing ignorance and death. White alone is the promise of the resurrection, immortality, life; and Jesus wore it, as did the angels when they appeared to the Marys and the disciples. If the Church believes what it preaches, let it begin by teaching that white alone should be worn as the symbol of eternal life, ignoring black as well as death. Or let ordinary dress be worn rather than formal black, which is so oppressive and depressing in its sinister umbrage and hopeless suggestiveness. These are but forms, very external and superficial, it is true, but trailing clouds of doubt and despair rather than glory and revelation. These outward shows of grief are only mentioned because nowhere except among Christians is black used on occasions of mourning. For Turkey, which is Mohammedan, wears violet ; China, which is Buddhistic and Shintoistic, white ; Egypt, which is Mohammedan, Arabic, and Jewish, yellow. Black was once used considerably in the Orient. Now it has passed to the Christian Occident, and it is to be hoped that it will be displaced by white, or no particular colour at all, as positive, scientific proofs of the soul's immortality become widely accepted.

Among the Druids and early Celts it was taught that nature had endowed every form of life with a specialized instinct or intelligence. Professor Agassiz expressed it by the word "teleology." This instinct guides each form of life in a particular way. It is not omniscient, but sufficient for its needs. Man seems to rise above the limitation and necessity of this specialization, and has powers which prognosticate limitless unfoldment and possibilities. No one sense or faculty or their expressions can exhaust consciousness. Divinity touches a high level in man's consciousness, and swings the arc of illumination more inwardly upon the self. And this is the lesson and the greater revelation of the life of Jesus Christ. He boldly declared, "I am the resurrection and the life," despite Jewish agnostic and materialistic doctrines of a future life. His teaching was gnostic, not nescient. The knowledge of the resurrection was vital to life itself. Life is a denial of death, of nescience. It is a revelation of power, an onward, forward, upward movement of the spirit. The resurrection is life in all its potentiality, making for its highest and best, the spiritual, the divine.

When and how is this gnosis or knowledge to come? Does it endow one with power to live and be? The knowledge of the resurrection comes by the expression of the life and intelligence on inner, subjective, subliminal planes, where the new moon of spiritual realities is first seen as a slender crescent rising above the ocean of material life; and secondly, by each one realizing that he is *in* the world, but not *of* it. In other and plain words, making one conscious of one's immortality, and, therefore, by an expression of the supernormal powers, enumerated (but not categorically) by Paul in the twelfth chapter of the Corinthians, wherein be speaks of spiritual gifts. This psychic training, supplemented by the spiritual life, would lift the soul out of materialism and afford abundant evidences of eternal life, and the inlook upon the future as well as the outlook upon life for which such transcendent and supersentient powers exist. If the world grieves or mourns, it is possibly because it is without such knowledge and development of powers. If it has not the true focus of life, and fails to realize the purpose of human experience and destiny, it is because of ignorance of the inner, upward rise or resurrection of the soul. This would not have been so, nor should it be so, under the discipline and principles which Jesus exacted as necessary and fundamental to what is termed the spiritual life. The attempted separation and divorce of supernormalism from spirituality of life is, without doubt, the cause of the bankruptcy and materialism of the Christian world and Church. Supernormalism does not imply magical or supernatural use of power, but the higher expression of normal power, correspondential with the ascending life of the soul and the purpose of the resurrection thus affording the basis of mystical facts upon which to rest one's campaign against agnostic and false teachings which are wholly materialistic in their claims and proofs. This use of supernormalism—call it by any other rational and intelligible name one chooses—is what gave Christian Science its numbers of adherents, because the logical assumption is that if Jesus healed by his Divinity, mankind can do the same. And the only apology, if such is necessary, for the Christian Scientist to offer for the Christian Science Church gradually superseding the Christian Church is that the one does not recognize Divinity in all mankind as a working hypothesis of healing and re-creation, while the other does!

The same might apply to all the spiritual powers enumerated by Paul, which, instead of being employed as they should be as the fruits as well as spiritual weapons of the spirit, have been consigned to charlatans, astrologers, fortune-tellers, who have exploited them as antichrist and as money-making schemes. The spiritualist medium and the psychic are not and should not be put in this class, except as they practise fraud or allow their powers to be used for selfish and commercial purposes. No amount or consolidation of organization can avail the truth if it is defeated by a body of Spiritualists, Christians, Christian Scientists, Theosophists, and New Thoughters who fail to live it. A spiritualist medium is on a par with the Christian clergyman who sacrifices truth or a spiritual life for professionalism. Spiritualism is no more to be considered the spurious brand labelled so by the public, and made such by ignorant camp-followers of untrained, illiterate, selfish, and often bogus mediums, than the cant, hypocrisy, the false theology, of some Christian clergymen are to be accepted as genuine and Simon-pure Christian teaching and life. The worthy everywhere suffer because of the unworthy, and the author of this book would be the last to judge or misjudge anyone who, whether in or out of the Church, squares his teaching and profession with his life. The facts remain, and they stubbornly resist concealment. They expose the rottenness of a condition which needs mending. They indict not truth, nor Christianity as taught and lived by the founder, nor his sincere and noble followers, not Spiritualism, nor mediums, seers, or psychics, who sacrifice their all for their convictions, revelations, and scientific demonstrations of immortality, and seek to put into practice the ideals of the higher education, but the bigoted ignoramus, the egotist, illiterate, the partisan, the hypocrite, the professional, the vicious, who masquerade before the world as saintly adherents and chosen oracles, but whose knowledge, power, understanding, life, and works prove their unworthiness, impositions, and pretensions. All this has damaged the cause before the world and in the eyes of the enlightened, and yet truth has survived to lead the free soul to the fullness of knowledge and understanding.

So, removing such obstacles as have stood in the way of public prejudice against and the appreciation of supernormalism, and strongly advising that it has nothing whatever to do with "mediumship," "supernaturalism," "magic," "fortune-telling," "necromancy," "palmistry," and "astrology," the subject of communing with the spirit world, as the supreme comfort of twentieth-century science and religion, can be approached as the most natural thing in the world.

The aspiration to commune with our loved ones who have passed through the change called death is abundantly shared by them. No one knows the efforts and struggles they have made and are making to reach and notify us of their survival. Modern Spiritualism, as having only to do with the soul's survival of death, is a world *movement*, showing that the human race is upset by these abnormal and supernormal phenomena. They are difficult to comprehend. Now that thousands have been slaughtered by the European War, and as many homes have been made desolate, the interest in the spirit people and world will be greater than ever.

Need it be said that the same sight, hearing, and feeling which psychologists call normal can be so extended as to unfold and express what the New Psychologists term the "supernormal," which means that the gifts or powers known as "discerning of spirits"—that is, spiritual (clairvoyant) seeing, spiritual (clairsentient) feeling, spiritual (clairaudient) hearing—can connect us in spirit communication with the so-called dead? Is it less honourable and respectable to-day to do so than it was in the days when Jesus, Peter, and Paul practised these gifts of the spirit? Did not Paul say in his defence before King Agrippa, "I was not unfaithful to the heavenly vision"? Because the vision was that of the Master, was it less a vision and more to be respected or obeyed than the helpful counsel of mother or father who appear also in vision to warn and to guide? Is not God in minimum as well as maximum where two or three are gathered together in His name, to dwell in communion of spirit and for greater service? If Paul heard the voice of Jesus, might not you or I hear the voice of sainted loved ones or those to whom the law of attraction draws us? Joan d'Arc heard the voices, and through them she led Charles to victory. She was a shepherdess, yet the voices of certain saints spoke to her clairaudient ear just as other and as saintly voices may speak to us. Nature has endowed us with these supernormal faculties, which have their external sense and organic functions on the physical side of life and outlets into the physical world, and it is for us to express and realize them here and now, to follow the soul as it passes through the valley and the shadow of death, and so, without losing one's interest in or depreciating life or dwelling too often in the "upper room" of the spirit, to walk the holier and happier in the light of this supreme revelation of the resurrection.

CHAPTER IV

The Evils and the Dangers of Inhibiting These Supernormal Faculties—The Good and the Benefits of Unfolding Them

In order to appreciate the uses to which the supernormal powers can be put, it will be wise to remind the reader of the two classes of psychical phenomena with which the New Psychology deals. One class is called abnormal, which is the abnormal use of supernormal powers; and the other is supernormal, which is normal power extended beyond sense limitations. The word "abnormal" should never be mistaken for "subnormal," nor made its equivalent, for the word "abnormal" as here employed has no relation whatsoever to mental deficiency or moral delinquency. And here, lest the class of psychic phenomena called "abnormal" be misunderstood, misprized, or adjudged of no particular value as bearing upon the problem of the soul's discarnated existence, the two words "medium" and "mediumship" must be mentioned, as making such phenomena possible. It may be asked, "What are such phenomena?" Any phenomenon, as the word signifies by derivation, is merely an appearance. Whether the phenomenon is natural or psychic, its substance is shadowy—that is, a form or an appearance. To entitle a phenomenon to be called psychic, it must be an appearance of soul—that is, a manifestation of the soul. And to qualify a psychic phenomenon as abnormal, it must occur in an unusual, unnatural way. Now abnormal psychic phenomena occur in the presence of mediums, through an organic sensitiveness which, for the lack of a more intelligible word, is called mediumship. Mediums are not subnormal people, neither insane, degenerate, nor criminal, and yet through the ages no class of men and women have been more abused, misunderstood, slandered, and criminally hounded and persecuted, even martyred.

Strange as it may seem, they are not responsible for these psychic phenomena which transpire in their presence. There are two kinds of mediums, the normal and trance; and two classes of mediumistic phenomena, physical and mental. The normal or trance medium may receive both physical and mental phenomena. Need it be said here that the spirit world project these phenomena by a law of control which neither science nor the New Psychology has as yet explained? That these phenomena do occur, science has conceded. Sir Oliver Lodge, in a recent address, declared, "We ourselves are not limited to a few years that we live on earth. We go on without it. We certainly continue to exist. We certainly survive. Why do I say that? I say it on definite, scientific grounds. I say it because I know that certain friends of mine still exist, because I have talked to them. Communication is possible. One must obey the laws and find out the conditions. I do not say it is easy, but I say it is possible; and I have conversed with them, as I could converse with anyone in this audience. . . . I tell you, that it is so with all the strength of conviction I can muster—that it is so; that we do exist; that people still take an interest in things going on; that they still help us, and know more about things than we do, and that they are able from time to time to communicate with us. . . . I tell you that we are surrounded by beings working with us, co-operating and helping, such as people in visions have had some perception of, and that which religion tells us saints and angels are." Sir Oliver Lodge obtained much of his evidence through mediums whose abnormal phenomena convinced him that he was communicating with his spirit friends. As an astute scientist and physicist, his word is not only convincing, but authoritative. Much of his evidence came through trance or semi-entranced mediums, who, whether altogether unconscious of what was given through them or not, made it possible for him to talk with spirit people.

The public is not generally informed on the subject of the trance, and there seems to be a profound mystery about it. The word literally means "to go across." The trance implies a sleep. Consciousness and unconsciousness imply conditions. All normal people live in the objective consciousness. When we supernormalize our mind, and key certain faculties, as seeing, hearing, and feeling, to supernormal vibrations, we enter the subjective mind, and into this mind the medium is taken, who passes into a trance by the will of a controlling or manifesting spirit. Often the trance is so deep and unconscious that the mediums are not aware of what takes place in their presence, or of the thoughts they utter; and it often happens that their own personalities or spirits are displaced by the operating intelligences; while in other cases they are overshadowed. In this condition it not infrequently happens that our loved ones on the spirit side talk through the medium, using the medium's brain and vocal organs, giving messages or affording convincing tests of their identity. Often the controlling intelligence is the spokesman, for not every spirit is skilled in the science of spirit communication. For this science must be studied and learned as any other science, and it stands to reason that some are more proficient in it and have a peculiar fitness for it. Oftentimes the message is written by automatic writing—that is to say, the arm and hand are only controlled, and what is written is not at all of the mind or desire of the medium. Again, the writing can occur independently, between slates screwed together or on tablets of paper, while the medium may be engaged in ordinary conversation, quite unconscious of the writing. The author of this book has had over two hundred such writings, in English, Greek, and Latin, and the writing has occurred on slates suspended from the chandelier and in broad daylight, and also while holding a book slate before a tent in the open air. The most common methods employed by the spirit world in reaching those still in the physical form is through the trance, clairvoyance, clairaudience, automatic and slate writing, ballot messages, and physical phenomena, culminating in materializations when spirits reclothe themselves temporarily in matter to give scientific demonstrations of their presence in a body, to prove to the agnostic or doubter that they once inhabited the body. In all such phenomena the most exacting test conditions have been enforced with remarkably startling results.

Such mental and physical phenomena are abnormal, because the result of the will of the discarnated spirits through mediums.

Not everyone is a medium. In fact, statistics show that not one out of fifty thousand of persons is a medium. But many are called mediums who are really psychics.

A medium is a psychic, but a psychic is not necessarily a medium.

A psychic is one who uses supernormal powers, not abnormally as mediums do, but as anyone uses normal powers, naturally, as we say, and without the trance or without being controlled or obsessed by spirits.

Frequently, under misguidance, a person who is not a medium will sit for the development of one or another phase of mediumship, and, after a protracted time, will fail; whereas had he put into practice certain simple but fundamental rules for supernormal development, he would have succeeded.

The two words "supernormal" and "abnormal" are very dissimilar when applied to the use of the same powers, and one who is a psychic cannot hope to become a medium or develop mediumship if not born so.

A medium is born; a psychic is unfolded. What is unfolded in man which qualifies him as a psychic? The man *plus* is man as the psychic, conscious of his Divinity and expressing his supernormal powers, but the man only is the potential psychic, unaware of latent Divinity and unexpressed supernormal faculties.

The entire burden of the teachings and the works of Jesus was laid upon the supernormal use of Divinity in the normal world and life. He declared that one should be in the world, but not of it. Daily transfigured by a host of heavenly witnesses, this vision became an inspiration to courage, a comfort in his loneliness, and an assurance that the cross would lead to the crown. Scoffed at by the mob of howling, coarse, vulgar, and low-browed materialists and Pharisees, his refined soul could still rise to the subliminal consciousness and give proofs of his Divinity in his patience, resignation, and silence. "They know not what they do." Stoning a prophet was a pleasing occupation of organized authority, masquerading in the robes of rabbi, priest, soldier, ruler, or king. But they all lacked the spirituality and supernormal development of the Prophet Jesus of Nazareth, and hence he forgave them. They were incapable of knowing what they did. They were, of a truth, insane. Sane, they called themselves; but is anyone sane who is not supernormally unfolded? To inhibit the expression of one's supernormal powers is to belie the life, stunt one's growth, and mock one's destiny. It is to open the flood-gates of animalism and sensuality, and to hobnob with the swine. It is to eat, drink, and be merry, for to-morrow we die. It is to blot out the morning star of hope and the evening star of promise of eternal life. And yet how there can be spirituality and not the exercise of the spiritual gifts enumerated by Paul, how one can be spiritual and yet inhibit the supernormal in his life, is one of the mysterious and almost inexplicable anomalies associated with the Christian life! How one can live a so-called Christian life and not see clairvoyantly and hear clairaudiently, as Paul saw and heard Jesus, is very strange. Where are the dead, that these purified and beatified Christians do not see and hear them as of yore? They are alive, and are not in their graves waiting the resurrection dawn of doomsday. The average Christian, trained and hypnotized to believe (not know) that their dead are asleep in the grave or in their Lord, which is one and the same, are dumb, deaf, and blind to their appeal from the spirit world. In the grave "Look for him not," said the angel of the Christ, "for he is risen." So your dead are not in their graves; they too have risen, are alive, and are pleading with you to welcome them again and anew in your arms—but in another condition: with tears and pains all gone, happy for ever!

If there is any efficacy, as we know there is, in suggestion, the Catholic Church is psychological, to say the least, in placing before the mind's eye of their communicants a male image of Joseph, the earthly father of Jesus, for the females, and a female image of Mary, the earthly mother of Jesus, for the males, in order to attract the spirits of Joseph and Mary to them. If there is any science in the art of conjuration, this is the method of conjuration the Catholic Church employs. On the other hand, the

Spiritualist and student of the New Psychology need employ no concrete idols or images to attract their loved ones who have passed beyond the veil. Such crude idolatrous use of facts is for vulgar and ignorant folk, not for enlightened men and women. And yet beneath and back of it is a universal law which makes for and governs all democratic spirit communications. There are and can be no exceptions to the rule, because if the law makes it possible for Jesus, Joseph, and Mary to appear to the lowliest souls on earth who visualize through their crude images the fashion and appearance of their spirits when on earth, surely any soul who will, and who will make conditions possible for spiritual communion and communication, can come *en rapport* with their spirit loved ones.

Briefly, these supernormal powers with which each one is endowed can and should be unfolded. Not to do so—that is, ignorantly or deliberately to inhibit them—will produce obsessions of a greater or less degree of violence, ill health, insanity, and other abnormal, pathological conditions ; while to develop them will qualify one to know himself, which is the greatest knowledge attainable. It will furnish him with unimpeachable divine guidance. It will show him life as it is, in the light of conditions which must pass away. It will show him the sweet purpose of pain and divine ministry of sorrow. It will reveal one's work and vocation in the light of duty and destiny. It will uncover the hidden steps of the blind alleys of human progress, and, throwing a light upon them, show that there is nothing hidden nor occult except to the unillumined. The sick will see the cause of their diseases, and be given the knowledge and power to heal themselves. One will learn how to make true friends, avoid enemies and danger, prepare for contingencies and crises, when to make journeys—in short, how to live peaceably and happily. The inventor and poet will be in conscious touch with those great souls on the spirit side who serve humanity through inventive genius. Scientists will be able to connect spirit with matter, and biology and physiology, as well as geology and anthropology, with psychology, ontology, and revelation. Education will cease to be merely physical and of the earth earthly; it will deal with life which is potentially divine, and with knowledge which reduces waste, speculation, and experiment to a minimum. Wealth and business as now exploited, with its warlike instincts for survival and possessions, will pass from earth as a human curse and pestilence, and the terrific struggle for existence will be no more, for the love of truth and the pursuit of wisdom will engage and enthral man's powers. To possess wealth and pursue business for material pleasure and aggrandizement will be looked upon as a curse, and the occupation of the subnormal. Supernormalism will create and define the superman, and our present military autocracy or democracy will be a thing of the past.

How all this will come to pass will be evident to all who are able to peer into the vistas of the future which supernormalism has opened to our clairvoyant vision. Inhibition of supernormal power is not conservation, but a personal detriment. The programme of life covers not a phase of life, but all of life. The plan is nccessary to the building of the foundation. Such plan is not a concoction of experience. It is a revelation. This conception of the plan is as old as Midian Masonry, and conceives of exact mathematical knowledge, governing all our steps. This plan, whether revealed by a master intelligence who knows how to build the perfect temple, or to workmen who only know how to do the work assigned them, is without error. Accidental births, under this plan, would be impossible.

In the problems touching the soul's immortality the inhibition of supernormal powers is a reactionary influence on one's health, by closing the doors of spiritual inspiration and influence and prejudicing one's mind to the revelations of the higher life. The doctrine of " one world at a time " is a fool's philosophy. This life is temporal, it is true; but unless fundamentally preparatory to the higher, spiritual, it is a loss. Rudolph Steiner, a German Theosophist, makes bold to say that one can no more expect to see on the spirit side of life by inhibiting that sight now—that is, making no conditions for its expression—than a baby can expect to see whose eyes have not been fashioned in its mother's womb. And startling as such fact is, the New Psychology proves that clairvoyance is as much a necessary faculty of our present existence as it is to be after death. It is our present physical seeing expressing itself beyond physical and sense limitations, and who would deny that such extension is not most valuable? Physical science has aided medical science by showing the tremendous importance of the X-ray in surgery, the violet ray in the treatment of cancer, and special forms of electrical energy in the treatment of certain nervous disorders and other diseases. And need it be said that such discoveries in physical science would not have been made possible had it not been for the inspirations and guidance of spirits, spirit photography, and such works as *Transcendental Physics*, by Zollner, who was a spiritualist and a pioneer psychical researcher. Not by inhibiting but by exhibiting supernormal power Sir William Crookes has advanced his scientific investigations. Do you not know that our brethren on the spirit side have as profound an interest as ever in our physical as well as spiritual well-being, and that they are doing their utmost to reach us? What are we doing if we shrink from the task, shirk our duty, and refuse even to unlock the closed but not forbidden door of the soul which leads us to the more excellent way of life of which Paul spoke? If man would give one-third as much attention to the investigation and practice of supernormal powers and development, revelations and demonstrations of a most helpful and convincing quality and quantity would be gotten. Of course, this is the real difficulty in the way of a thorough and comprehensive knowledge of the subject.

The average man will tell you he has not the time or the disposition to give to such study and practice, and, consigning the investigation of it to psychology experts, will abide by their possibly prejudiced, narrow, and superficial conclusions, as has been the case with certain Boards or Commissions relative to the disposition of certain huge sums of money left for the investigation of Spiritualism by devout advocates. Often such persons will brush aside enormous proven data for theological doctrines of the resurrection, as though modern evidence of the soul's immortality had nothing whatever to do with true or false claims of the resurrection as presented by the Christian Church. Science, eclectic education, unfettered and unbought men and women, those who dare think for themselves, are slowly destroying institutions, public opinion entrenched in certain interests, newspaper cant, and sectarian prejudice that abet the old decadent order of things against the spiritually new; and these are the most hopeful signs of the times. Truth will not down. Facts stubbornly challenge and demand acceptance. Theorize as one may, an ounce of demonstration is worth a ton of belief.

Supernormal experiences are not matters of belief, but facts. Failing eyesight and hearing can be traced to a lack of unfoldment of clairvoyant and clairaudient deficiencies. To develop one's supernormal power of seeing is not only to illumine the consciousness, but to clarify the sense of sight; and as proof, cases of pure, clear eyesight and eyes in which there are no cloudy or dull effects belong to those who can see clairvoyantly, whether they are conscious of it or not.

Deafness is no bar to clairaudience, and yet persons whose hearing is acute and continues acute into old age are those who hear voices—the voice of the soul; in short, are those who are clairaudient.

Could the spirit thus express itself from centre to circumference, from the conscious subjective to the conscious objective mind, who will deny that the supernormal seeing, hearing, and feeling would not finally displace the physical altogether, with the result that purer men and women, in finer bodies, would people the earth? We pay the penalty for any and all inhibitions of spiritual power with diseased bodies and minds and miserably unhappy lives. Time may heal all wounds, as the saying goes; but memory and conscience never sleep, and they point to our imperfect, unfinished, and dissatisfied lives until death proves to us that there were many things which we left undone which ought to have been done, and many things done which ought to have been left undone. The instinct for life is exceeded only by the greater longing for immortality. And if this longing is to be expressed or unexpressed, the expression must not be some belief, however time-honoured, nor some vague, indefinite, unprovable promises based upon human opinion, but facts which each one may know for himself. And what will be a holier urge or a nobler inspiration to present duties and living than the knowledge which supernormalism affords through our own Divinity, that each lesson of life is a step toward the apex of the pyramid of spiritual realities, where doubts end and certainties begin? And this is so. For such knowledge may come to us early or late in life, by birth or through struggle; but when it comes it clears away the mists, and we see things as they are. To inhibit such powers as open up the mind to the consciousness of these spiritual realities is to foredoom life to despair. With an intellectual and moral culture such as this present life can afford, broad, aesthetic, and felicitous as it is, the soul is dissatisfied, as is proven by the universal unrest, decadence of the Church, and of the increase of crime, insanity, and degeneracy. The simple life among cultured people means either a fortune to live up to the ideal, or among the less fortunate a struggle to be against the high cost of living, and a gradual submergence among the vulgar. But with the vision opened upon the spiritual world self-denial becomes easy, service makes the vulgar our friends, and, as Cardinal Newman expressed it, "The physical possessions of this earthly life dwindle into insignificance." For to know the foundation as well as elements of that culture which unfold the soul in fullest expansiveness of life and service is to be qualified to live and enjoy life. To this end supernormalism calls us. Not to die, but to live; but so to live that we shall know the truth concerning this life and the life that is to come.

CHAPTER V

Specializing Supernormal Powers to Obtain Evidences of our Immortality and Divinity

In an experience covering over twenty years the author has found no college or school outside of "The College of Divine Sciences and Realization" where supernormal powers or faculties can be and are specialized. This college is not a group of buildings located in any city, but a correspondence school, which has been in existence since 1893. It is a pioneer institution of its kind, and antedated the publications of the Psychical Research Society and the monumental work, entitled *The Human Personality and Its Survival of Death,* by the late Dr. Frederic Myeis. True, esoteric societies existed among the Theosophists for the promulgation and practice of such teaching, but no scientific system was taught openly for the expression of psychic and supernormal powers. As a matter of fact, the Theosophical Society until very recently made very little of supernormal powers.

During the past twenty years only a few books appeared on the subjects, and most of these books sprung into existence at long intervals, covering the last ten years. Mediumistic circles or circles for the development of the various phases of mediumship were common, but that development should never be confounded with supernormalism. The literature on the direct subject of supernormal development is exceedingly meagre, and confined to a few authors; chiefly because only the free, courageous, and pioneer souls dared to publish such books at the risk of ignorant and violent criticism and financial loss. However, while there is more demand to-day for literature on occult science (an increase of two hundred per cent. in ten years) and for text-books on how to express one's supernormal powers, the difficulties in the way of successful practice are the same as ever.

The text-books have spiritually and scientifically revealed the principles. Man has been slow, very slow indeed, in putting these principles into practice. In some cases expert advice proved unnecessary, as the text-books covered the science even to the experimental part of such psychic development. However, as expert advice is never untimely, it might be well to offer the student of supernormal development some suggestions which have proven very helpful to the author and his numerous students. For to specialize any of our supernormal faculties requires not only a knowledge and a wide experience of technical rules, but careful observation of and attention to each possible change in the minds of students who are applying such rules. And as no two cases are alike, although results average the same, the general advice which may apply to one may not wholly apply to another, except with modifications.

First, the student must realize that when he is dealing with the soul he is dealing with immaterial substance ; that is, however material it is, essentially or absolutely, it is not physical matter. Therefore the results which he seeks cannot be sensed or perceived as ordinary normal experiences. The phenomena will not be physical, nor will they occur outside himself. It is a fact, though not widely believed or generally known, that, however objective or mental or physical material mediumistic phenomena are, they transpire through and because of the medium, the medium's mind first receiving them from the outside spirit intelligence. They are none the less genuine because this is so, nor does it follow that the medium should always be conscious of this fact. This can be further explained and made clearly intelligible by illustration. Our bodies are outside resemblances of our personalities, yet the body is physical and personality superphysical. Yet the correspondence no one will deny. It may not always be nicely fitted except in thought, surely not in laboratories, as clothes to one's body. A yet more subtile connection exists between the individuality and the personality, and yet the "I" or ego manifesting itself through them all is in form of resemblance superior in substance to the body, personality, and individuality. The subtile and illusive phenomena called supernormal consists of inspirations, visions, voices, and feelings which transcend mental processes and are not perceived by the normal mind or any of the normal faculties and senses, but are realized in the consciousness when supernormal powers are active. And these are the experiences which have been known under the various names of mystic, occult, religious, and spiritual, because no word describing physical experiences founded originally on sense perception and sensation could apply to or define them.

Again, when one specializes these psychic faculties, these uncommon experiences become as natural as any common experiences, and yet require a certain understanding of the law to adequately and intelligently express, perceive, and classify them. But if one knows in the beginning that these rare phenomena do not appear in physical form as the product of the objective mind, but in the consciousness of the subjective mind in objective form, then there will be no confusion of ideas as to where and how to find them, and their appearances will not bewilder one. The finer these phenomena of inspirations, visions, voices, and feelings, the more highly developed must one's spiritual nature be; for supernormal unfoldment concerns the spiritual rather than human nature, and as spiritual things must be spiritually discerned, heard, and felt, the advantage of careful, conscientious training will be evident. No one can hope to attain to this degree of illumination and conscious subjectification of normal powers in any given time, because time depends or waits upon practice. This caution is given because so few will patiently apply themselves even to such entrancingly exalting work unless the very faculties they are training begin to produce miracles. Need it be said that no miracles should be expected or will appear? The process itself is slow because carefully and exactingly unfolded.

For some time memory pictures may appear and be accepted as symbolic visions. It will be found, however, that in stilling or silencing the outward, sensuous, objective mind these pictures will appear until by concentration the ego is able to attract the pure subjective visions, which will differ from the memory pictures in the fineness and ethereality of their substance. Memory pictures, however artistic, are usually gross when compared with visions.[1]

Often the life force has become scattered and weakened by desultory thinking and the material life, and this behaviour has made concentration either difficult or impossible. Restraining one's self, though necessary, until self-control is attained is assisted greatly by the more positive love of the work of unfoldment itself. To enter upon this work with earnestness and sincerity of purpose, allowing neither pleasure nor physical interests to distract the mind or draw one away from times sacredly set for silent meditation and aspiration, is to form conditions for the happiest concentration. As a direct result of this mental attitude and concentration a conservation of mental and vital forces follows. A sublime optimism inspires the

[1] If the student is unfamiliar with scientific and spiritual methods of supernormal development, it will be very helpful to him to study thoroughly Judge Troward's *Edinburgh Lectures on New Thought*, also *Clairaudience* and *Clairvoyance*, by J. C. F. Grumbine, and apply experiments.

soul. Ability to enter upon other lines of work with enthusiasm displaces diffidence and indifference, because all work now is so placed as not to dissipate the forces nor obsess the mind, but is the natural flow of one's life along the path of duty and service. The brain waxes strong in grey matter as the mind is more centred and the ego polarized, and the general health improves because there is no leakage or waste. The light of the soul from its innermost centre has now the conditions for free radiation, and in consequence of this change in the mental attitude the soul can pursue its inner spiritual pilgrimage.

It is not necessary for one to be an expert in psychology in order to reach the subjective sphere of the spirit where spiritual evidences of immortality are obtainable. It is only necessary that one conscientiously apply certain technical rules and conditions, and in good faith live the moral life necessary to make that technique efficacious.

Now, aside from the positive assurances of personal evidences of immortality or the survival of the human personality of death given us by the Psychical Research Society in their records and its ablest members in their published books, lectures, and interviews, and by Theosophists and Spiritualists the world over, the average agnostic and investigator wishes to know for himself. He does not deny the enormous bulk of such evidence and its value, but he pleads for individual proof. To all such there is and can be but one answer. Know yourself. It is your duty to know, and, what is best of all, the proof is within your reach. For, as fully explained, supernormalism is a subject of investigation and proof, but supernaturalism is not. No individual proof can be had of the alleged supernaturalism of the Bible. Its own statements of facts must be accepted or rejected *prima facie,* or the same facts rationalized or explained by another word than supernaturalism. Not so, for instance, with the supernormal faculty of seeing, called also prescience, clairvoyance, seership, second sight, and prevision, and the supernormal faculties of hearing, so remarkably developed in Joan d'Arc, the Maid of Orleans, and clairsentience, which is a basic psychic faculty upon which the other two are built. Spiritual evidences of our own divinity as well as our own immortality are realized through these powers. The near beyond is made so near that we can see the beckoning hands and hear the voices of our loved ones. Experimentally and scientifically, when once the sight is cleared and the fog lifted, the spirit world can bring us unmistakable evidences of their presence. For consciousness, though conditioned by our objective mind, very much as the objective mind, so far as consciousness is concerned, is conditioned by sleep, is free to reflect the visions of the spirit world when once the objective conditions—that is, the mind—is for the time silenced or put to sleep. Unconscious we shall not become, but we shall inhibit the action of the objective while we exhibit passively the subjective mind. And this will be done so gradually and truly, because such growth is gentle and silent, that we shall daily see an extension and sublimation of the vision, and so obtain the results we seek. The objective mind is the sphere of action, but an action which is dynamic—that is, destructive—for the outward is mortal—that is, always changing and dying. The subjective mind is the sphere of passivity, but a passivity which is static—that is, constructive—for the spiritual is ethereal. To polarize or centralize the ego in consciousness, it is necessary to lift it above the sordid, gross, sensual things of the earth life. To do so, more than thinking of spiritual things or putting into practice technical rules of supernormal development is necessary. The spiritual life must precede all theoretic practice, or the results will be doubtful. When the student has attained to a degree of discipleship where master and servant are exchangeable and equivalent terms, and can unselfishly and abstemiously surrender himself to the call of the spirit, initiation into the sublime mysteries of the spiritual kingdom will follow. This is the more excellent way, even though the way of solitude, for the pilgrim is on his way to the Holy City of Light, and that city cannot be entered save as he is a light-bearer, as Jesus expressed it in the parable of the Five Foolish and Five Wise Virgins. The soul appears as a mere shadow in consciousness, until that consciousness is filled with its effulgent light; then the shadow disappears and the soul's illumination dawns.

Supernormal evidences of one's immortality are of two kinds. One kind deals with the expression of the supernormal powers as revealed in spirit communion, and the other with the mystical experiences which touch our own Divinity. The phenomena of these two classes are closely interwoven. Sometimes it is difficult to separate them. For instance, divine guidance through wisdom and understanding as revealed by the oracle of intuition, or the voice of God as revealed in conscience, can be obeyed implicitly, and yet generally the visions and voices of spirits agree with the vision and voice of God. The reader must continually bear in mind that in speaking of God, the Highest Self, and our Divinity the author makes no distinction. They are one and the same, so that the realization of one's Divinity means precisely what Jesus meant when he said, "I and the Father are One." Usually, God is supposed to be externalized and separated from one's Divinity, and is not an immanent Presence. On the other hand, abundant evidences can be cited to show that Divinity is potential in us all—in fact, in everything. So that if divine guidance from within each soul is possible, whether incarnate or excarnate, then, all other things being equal, there should be a perfect agreement between souls. Error is possible when one's opinions or impressions, based largely on one's personal experiences or convictions, are offered instead of divine guidance. Temperamentally, we are conditioned, and the particular and numerous experiences we enjoy are what they are largely because of temperament, as the ray of light is coloured by the stained glass through which it passes. Truth as revealed in each one's soul is, however, absolute.

The mystical experiences of class two are the deepest and most difficult to analyse, because there can be no higher or comparative experiences of a similar class. In the consciousness called "subliminal," super, and cosmic, both supernormal and mystical experiences have their birth. Once attain to this consciousness by concentration, meditation, and abstemiousness, and these mystical and supernormal experiences follow.

Now there is not a person who does not know what it means to follow his conscience, that still small voice of divine guidance with which all are endowed. And surely every woman knows the value of intuition, even if it is not always obeyed. Such guidance is usually spoken of as the *vox dei* (voice of God), and is sufficient. But these far-away and yet omnipresent admonitors of life are not ordained to be the general utility functions. Intuition and conscience both have their offices—one to furnish divine guidance to the intellect, the other the same guidance to the heart or emotional nature. Their evidences are sufficient to prove the spiritual character of the soul and our Divinity.

To prove, however, that we can touch the near end of the spirit world, and have unmistakable evidences of our own immortality and that of our departed friends, we must supernormalize our expressions of consciousness, so that when we see, hear, or feel we shall dwell on and in the periphery of the consciousness, unconditioned by the physical senses or objective mind. And in this subliminal and subjective state of consciousness, spirit communion will be afforded.

The one who considers the attainment worth while will diligently and patiently seek it, and never shrink from temporary delays or the usual tests which try anyone who is not willing to remain on lower levels of life. For this consciousness, though it is uncreate, still will not manifest itself unless we love it and its sphere of light more that we do the physical things of time and sense.

First, let the student remember that he can enter this state of consciousness by sensitizing his body and mind, thus making it possible for him to become impressed, susceptible, and receptive to spirit presence and guidance. This can be done best by placing the body in a negative and the mind in a passive condition. Simple as this seems, it is most difficult to attain, for the normal hereditary body is full of fleshly lusts which need uprooting, and in order to do this the normal life must be spiritualized. This is done by purification and unselfishness. The best technique of supernormal psychology for the realization of this state of consciousness is valueless and useless unless one live a pure and unselfish life. In order to do this one is not compelled to be an ascetic. Purification will lead to dietetics—that is, a rechemicalization of the nerve centres, called in Hindoo philosophy "the tatwics," by a change in diet. Less and a different quality and combination of food will be chosen, and each one in process of psychic development will be impressed as to what to eat. Of course, no stimulants, condiments, tobacco, or liquors should be used. No one can hope to sensitize the cells of the body—in short, etherealize the organism—who will not rigidly obey first principles.

Under such régime there is no abrupt change. The change is slow and gradual, and therefore the student is required to be obedient and patient. The spiritual apprenticeship precedes initiation, but that apprenticeship is neither long nor short, quick nor slow, as we measure time and natural processes of growth, but a process altogether dependent upon ourselves. When the body becomes negative, the same condition is reached as a sensitized photographic plate. It does not mean that the person's body or organism is now more easily obsessed or controlled. On the contrary, the spiritual life lifts his attractions to that sphere of service where the spirit of co-operation obtains, and because of this spirit of self-possession, obsession becomes impossible. The will becomes freer as the soul becomes more centred in Divinity. This is the law of freedom and sovereinty. Passivity of mind follows, although it is a part of the general system of acquiring self-control of one's mental faculties and physical forces, so as to conserve the nervous and vital forces and turn them into grey matter with which to manifest the spirit on the higher planes of consciousness. As a lamp needs oil, as a match needs sulphur, or they cannot burn, so the grey matter of the brain is needed, at least on the physical and mental plane, to kindle supernormal manifestations. The brain becomes as the crystal sea touched with tongues of fires referred to by John in Revelation. When the life force, through the conservation of vitality, is sent up to the brain, then as one lives the spiritual life, which in itself is a process of regeneration and recreation, the mind settles into calm repose, and the ego, once distracted by illusions and estranged by vanities, now bows before the light that never was on sea or land, the light which is purely spiritual and which illumines the subjective mind and makes spiritual communion possible. Participation in this exalted sphere of consciousness depends upon one's consecutive daily habits of life. Pure and unselfish thoughts, sustained aspirations, meditations which involve not only willing self-examination, but thoughtful reflection upon the subject of spiritual worthiness, communion, and service, avail more than perfunctory sittings, burning of incense, mere formal prayers, or any occult ceremonials. If spirituality, with specialized sane and helpful rules, will not prove beneficial in involving the soul in its own Divinity, so as to be active clairvoyantly, clairaudiently, and clairsentiently—in plain words, to make spiritual communion between ourselves and our departed loved ones possible—then there can be no truth in Christian teaching.

This is the gnosis, the canonical teachings of the prophetic schools, the knowledge of the resurrection and the life, so vividly set forth in teaching and miracle and so calmly and divinely lived by Jesus. And, surely, if, as a result of the life he lived and the teachings he applied, he could say, "In my Father's house are many mansions," and "If it were not so, I would have told you," we all, figuratively speaking, can ascend the Mount of Transfiguration, and as he serenely communed with Elias and Moses, the prophet of Israel, so we can communicate with our beloved spirit friends.

CHAPTER VI

Death no Longer the End of Progress, nor the Limitation of Science

Since death has become a chemical and psychical change, in which the spiritual body is released from the physical simultaneously with the liberation of the spirit from its earthly environment, but in no sense affecting character or life nor disintegrating the personality, the word "progress" is big with meaning. Progress spiritually is neither linear nor vertical. Progress on the physical plane is manifestation (hence the word "phenomenon," an appearance), and on the mental plane it is expression (hence the word "neumenon," a realization). To go forward, as the word "evolution" suggests, is not the true meaning of manifestation, and yet all manifestations of life occur on successive, but not necessarily parallel planes. To be unfolded, as the word "education" implies, is to express oneself, and yet all expressions of intelligence lead out what is in you. Progress is dual in its purpose. If manifestation is, as it were, a reflection in a mirror, it is no less a link in the chain of physical causation and an evidence of growth. And yet the expression of the spirit governs its manifestation. As leaves of a tree point to the approach of fruit, so each natural manifestation of life toward a definite end. The expression and manifestation are simultaneous, but not similar, and both prophesy what is enfolded within the life itself. Here is the deeper application of the saying, "As a man thinketh, so is he." The body is the composite physical manifestation of what a man thinketh—that is, it expresses through his life intelligence and emotion. Progress is not a matter of any number or total of experiences, necessary as it is, but of destiny; and destiny is not only the active, vocational part one takes in life, but it is one's ambitions and ideals as shown in one's character. Now the spiritual part of destiny is that which leads to progress both in evolution and physical civilization, as well as in the character and life work of mankind. Not always manifest, the purpose of life sweeps along, shaping events and moulding environment to serve its high end.

If death ended progress, then there could be no meaning or purpose in the manifestations or expressions of life; but, inasmuch as death is neither a finality to progress, nor a differential in deciding or shaping one's destiny, but a providential change, the physical aspects of life hint through progress at large or small spiritual possessions both here and hereafter. These spiritual possessions gauge our real progress. So that, professionally and vocationally, the man may attain to a high degree of worldly excellence, and yet if, so far as his character is concerned, he remains unsympathetic, coarse, unlovable, miserly, unkind, cruel, brutal, he has made little or no progress here, and after death the state of his soul will be as low as his position on earth was high. This is what is meant by progress after death. Men often have honour, wealth, position, and name here, but in eternity, dishonour, poverty, ostracism, namelessness ; because on earth these words meant simply worldly honours, but in the spirit world of reality they stand not for shame, but for what we are. This is the meaning which modern revelations of spirit people give to the word "progress." Every step is a step upward. What we make of ourselves counts. Worldly standards, however, do not measure or determine our spirituality nor our spiritual stations.

Few of the old-school theologians still preach that the soul's fate is sealed at death, and that probation is for ever at an end ; but modernism, both in the Protestant and Catholic Church, insists, in accordance with well-established facts revealed by spirit people as to their life after death, that the soul's arc of progress ascends from darkness to light and from despair, remorse, sorrow, or loneliness to happiness. This is the most cheerful and hopeful message in connection with the positive proofs of the survival of the personal identity of death which has come to any generation, terrorized and tortured with threats of eternal damnation and the burning fires of hell. The dawn of the nineteenth and twentieth-century religion, no longer a religion of dogma and creed, but of science and love, is rosy with optimistic prophecies of universal peace! The European War, with its frightful, enormous toll of death and waste of billions of dollars' worth of property, sounds the death-knell not only of militarism, but of the militant Church, which sacrificed the cross for the sword, and made God an angry, revengeful Jehovah, instead of an all-wise, all-loving, all-just Spirit. So, with the destruction of militancy in Church and State, peace will follow, and the soil reddened by blood will soon bloom with the white lilies of the spiritual resurrection.

Across the borderland is a country as dear and near to every human heart as is home on earth, because there is not a home where there is not a vacant chair and some absent dear one who has crossed the great divide. That our loved ones are waiting for us is not only a reasonable belief, but a demonstrable fact, which has been proven over and over again. The mother waits and plans for her expectant babe with no more joy and sublime love than do our beloved spirit friends treasure dreams and thoughts of them and plan for our coming. And progress means not only our reunion, but, before we pass over, our ability to commune and communicate with them. For the former limitations placed upon science and the boundaries of human knowledge have disappeared in fact, faded away into an ever-widening, expanding sphere of unimagined and limitless revelation. We are not flippantly talking or writing to-day about "one world at a time" or *cui bono?* when duty points to psychical research, but are rather brushing our eyes, lest we may be asleep when still greater revealments of eternal life are discovered.

For the world in which we live is a microcosm after all, in which we have learned is located a macrocosm, which, as the little world is understood, reveals an occult passage-way into the greater world. Need it be said that this greater world is known to progressive souls only and shut out to all others?

The scientific and spiritual conceptions of progress do not differ radically. Practically and scientifically, progress becomes a synonym of expertness and efficiency, the ability to know and to do things of practical value, the fullest realization of power and intelligence along useful lines. Spiritually, it is moral expertness and divine efficiency, the ability to serve in a humanitarian sense, and so express the qualities of the spirit. A man can have either or both, but where both are combined in one man the greatest good is accomplished. Simply by living the practical life of an expert, without moral character or excellence, is as one-sided as is an intellectual life. Therefore one of the purposes of psychical research and knowledge is to show man how to progress—that is, to live on earth so that nothing will be left undone which should have been done, to cause regrets or disappointments on the immortal side of life. The point is admirably illustrated in low attractions or sectarian prejudices which here curtail one's usefulness and freedom, and on the spirit side make the soul earth and creed bound. Many reforms which ostensibly appear unrelated to spirit guidance and inspiration successfully fulfil their mission because they are sustained on earth by those who consciously or unconsciously are in direct touch with superior ministering and guiding influences. The emancipation of the slaves was such a reform, and President Abraham Lincoln admitted that he was led to sign his emancipation proclamation under spirit guidance. Great inventors are especially favoured by their superior helpers on the spirit side. Undoubtedly, the value of eugenics as a sweeping reformatory remedy of subnormality, in the form of defective mentality, crime, and degeneracy, was made possible by our brethren in the spirit world, who are busy impressing receptive minds what to do to improve and better human life and conditions. Progress is not theological, but a process of natural and spiritual evolution, eliminating all sumptuary, theological measures which reward right-doing and punish wrong-doing. Nature certainly abhors the dogmatic assumptions that she is revengeful. Cause and effect spurn theological cant and false inductions. Justice has in it neither a reward for righteousness nor a punishment for sin. Evil, so called, is a misnomer if it suggests any theological conception of natural or spiritual law which is a respecter of persons. So-called obedience to or violations of natural and spiritual law are effects which follow certain actions, and in the effects there is no element of reward or punishment. This element was introduced by theology to bolster up the doctrine of vicarious atonement. Once rewards of the righteous and punishments of the unrighteous extended indefinitely, and in the hereafter became fixed at death; but now law, as governing causes and effects, is remedial—that is, a blessing in disguise. The Buddhistic doctrine of karma, expressed in action—that is, whatsoever a man soweth, that will he reap—has gradually triumphed over the theological conceptions of rewards and punishments. The spirit world is unanimous in teaching this great fact of life, and the enormous mass of such testimony is sufficient guarantee that progress is in an ascending scale. Pain has its ministry, and sorrow its lessons, and experiences, however trying and bitter, their specific revelations. So it would be unwise to treat life on the physical plane as complete, and prejudice the mind in an agnostic way against the larger faith in the ultimate perfection and happiness of the human race.

Herbert Spencer declared that evil tends constantly to disappear, and in the sloughing-off process, despite the thin veneer of military civilization, the genuine qualties of manhood and womanhood are asserting themselves. The brutalizing and vulgarizing effect on character of this commercial and material age is everywhere apparent ; but that it will not last much longer, and will go down to oblivion as other such materialism has done, is warranted by the facts. The spirit of progress is readjusting fundamental canons or standards of right living on physical and spiritual planes ; and while the readjustment is necessarily slow because of sophisticated, false theological and unsound commercial doctrines which still influence the world's thought and life, the renaissance of a spiritual civilization in which the ideal of eternal progress and peace is at work is signally at hand. Life, like gold, is being tested by acid and fire. Dross and alloy are being detected and separated from the essential substance, and what endures is divine. It is this Divinity, call it by whatever name is synonymous, which determines the progress of the race, and science as well as philosophy are recognizing it as the only foundation on which humanity can build any enduring civilization.

To hypothecate the end of human progress at death, because of the alleged limitations of scientific knowledge of life after death, is presumptuous, to say the least, for enough evidence is at hand to prove that the soul progresses in the spiritual spheres, whatever may be its attractions or deterrents. It s this broad, but rational, natural, and demonstrable understanding of spirit life which robs death of its terror and affords a new vision of our earthly struggles!

Since science has found the spiritual hypothesis supremely tenable, its former severe, formidable, and hostile attitude to psychical phenomena has relaxed. And while it rejects supernaturalism, at the same time accepting supernormalism, it is finding that there is no abrupt chasm or interruption between physical (natural) and superphysical (spiritual) causality. This inlook upon life as it ascends the spiral staircase of invisible matter called ether is as promising a sign of scientific progress as the outlook upon life as it unfolds on the physical plane. And therefore death, instead of offering limitations upon science, spurs men of science on to greater efforts in penetrating the mysterious and semi-occult borderland which skirts our physical life and yet is, comparatively speaking, an undiscovered world.

All that we positively know of it is:

1. That it exists.

2. That it is the abode of spirit people, once inhabitants of earth.

3. That its life is as natural as our own.

Sir David Brewster, the English scientist, inspired and dominated by the restricted spirit of science, once declared that "spirits would be the last thing he would ever give in to," and yet it has been found that no other cause can be assigned to the production of abnormal phenomena than spirits. Spirits are individualized spirit ; and it is as plausible and scientific to accept the claims that our brethren on the spirit side do produce these abnormal phenomena in order to prove that they have survived the change called death, and can communicate (abnormally) as well as commune (supernormally) with us, as to stretch and pervert the facts to fit into some imaginary and undemonstrable hypothesis. This, modern science among the most enlightened and fearless advocates frankly admit. Who will deny that physical science is limited by physical apparatus? But who will dare to deny, in the face of all that has been revealed by psychical research, that science—that is, knowledge—will not be enormously increased by the use of our own superior subliminal faculties, which, in our enthusiastic idolatry of physical inductive methods and formulae, have been sadly neglected, if not inhibited? Progress along these lines as revealed by psychical science is necessary if the world is to be placed upon a plane where war will cease, civilization will not prove a phantom, and physical man will not revert to barbarism.

In ourselves as spirits we must find spirit, or Divinity, which some call God; and when this knowledge is revealed, progress toward the millennium will go forward in leaps and bounds, while error and superstition, entrenched in ignorance and creedanity, will die. Government will be self-government, while all other forms will pass away; and men will love each other, not for obtainment but attainment, not for business but fellowship. And if religion survives and even a relic of it remains, it will be service through the golden rule and guidance through conscience. Knowledge we shall all love, because it will improve us; while ignorance we shall spurn, because it will enslave us.

CHAPTER VII

THE UNIVERSE FOR MAN AND NOT MAN FOR THE UNIVERSE

THE geocentric idea of astronomy has been supplanted by the heliocentric, the sun, rather than the earth, becoming the centre of our universe. Whether the sun exists for the earth, or the earth exists for the sun, the fact remains that neither one could exist without the other. It is not conceit to think that man's existence and place in the universe are important enough to make possible the title of this chapter, "The Universe for Man and not Man for the Universe." Not that man is the lord or apotheosis of creation, but that in man, his life and consciousness, cosmology and cosmogony find their fullest expression and divinest fulfilment. Once man was A.B.C.; now he is X.Y.Z. *plus*—that is, he passes from the known to the unknown with greater prophetic possibilities and unlimited resources. Where, for instance, can human consciousness and intelligence be excelled? Surely not in any lower order of intelligence, among the subhuman kingdoms, wonderfully specialized and instructive with precocity as each form of life seems to be! The widest expanse, the deepest depth, and the highest reach of thought, so far as we know, is in man. Man at his best is now a submerged being, but so divinely endowed that deity seems within his grasp; not a perfected creature, but one in whom the elements of nature will yet so fuse as to polarize at length to fit him to be an angel. Soul unfoldment is a theme which furnishes continually inexhaustible material for spiritual growth and resurrections.

The ancients canonically placed the zodiacal signs or constellations around man, and framed him in a circle of 360 degrees. This is not only an inspiration, but a prophecy of his glory, achievement, and kingdom. All rays of light, not only the planetary, but the stellar, centre and fuse in him. He becomes the logos and the cosmos, the resurrection and the life. The purpose of life's travail and birth is the realization of consciousness and the life of one's Divinity. The electron, crystal, cell, germ, organism, the stone, the metal, the vegetable, life, all that encircles and enspheres the spirit of the universe, exist to declare man—

not human nature, but *ecce homo, ecce deus*!

The recent revival of the power of the human will over matter as well as life, a sort of new Christianity, which is leading man into incredible achievements over disease, infortune, even death; the breaking down of the walls which hitherto imprisoned the spirit and giving it power to express itself even after death—all show the involved purpose of the universe. Turn the universe inside out, and what have you? Surely not physical matter, held together by cohesion and adhesion, in a warp and woof of electrical energy, vitalizing the spinal column of the universe, but spirit, alive in a flame of light ineffably bright and eternal, and in which all objects stand up in their ethereal forms. Stange as it all may seem, the aura and emanations illustrate the degree of development and perfection of the particular life form. What is true of crystals and chemical substance, in which life manifests itself, is true of man. For the quality of life and the plane on which the individualized form of life functions determines the quality of light.

Now this divine test is what determines progress, for psychic unfoldment is clearly shown by the degree of luminosity and purity of the light, each soul radiating light according to its unfoldment. If Buddha and Jesus embody the Christos or Christ-principle of self-abnegation, finding one's Divinity in self-forgetfulness or human service, their spiritual light will be more brilliant than the sun; and Jesus himself, fully understanding the purpose of progress as applying to soul unfoldment, declared that "I am the light of the world." Christmas, the Epiphany, the Annunciation of the Virgin, the Transfiguration, the Resurrection, and the Ascension—all were manifestations of this Light which is the quality of the life, its degree of spirituality which permits this inner divine radiance, the God intelligence or spirit immanent in us to shine forth in all its ineffable glory. Race cycles and groups of kindred souls find their homogeneous sphere by this quality of development and light, as the ray of light refracts into its component primary reds, yellows, blues, and their complements.

Souls, undeveloped or developed, whether incarnate or excarnate, are thus placed in red, blue, yellow, violet, green, purple, brown, white vibrations; and these colours designate our psychic unfoldment or progress.

Psychic or spiritual unfoldment is progress, and this is the deeper, larger meaning of the word. Our stations or mansions, therefore, are determined by the development and perfection of the soul.

Now matter has always been considered, even in Eastern philosophy, a veil screening the spirit, a mere phenomenon of its inner reality. The Brahmins and Buddhists called it maya, an illusion. Low attachments and attractions make matter opaque and keep this veil black and impregnable, a veritable dungeon, in which the soul languishes; while self-renunciation liberates it and at once reasserts the nerve centres and rebuilds, as it recreates the cellular tissues to do the work and obey the command of the divine thought and will of the luminous spirit. This is what Jesus meant when he said, " Do not put new wine into old bottles.' Disease, degeneracy, and insanity, as results of mortal mind and beliefs in old bodies, are overcome, and the body becomes the spiritual vehicle of the spirit.

Such teaching would seem overwhelmingly gloomy and uninviting were it not for the fact that even the moral life—that is, the honest, virtuous, noble life—is the happiest, and produces the least friction or resistance. Pleasures and pain are of the senses, and are agreeable or disagreeable; and there is every reason for believing that it is no more a sin to live a natural life than it is a virtue to live the spiritual life, as it expresses itself through the senses. But the average man of the world, as well as the professional clergyman, think that the pleasures of the senses are for ever divorced from the category of spiritual assets. On the contrary, pleasure on its own plane is as worthy of our acceptance, if not made an end in itself or divorced from the spiritual life, as is happiness. At most it is a by-product of action; not a cause in itself, but an effect rather than a result. As such, it should be associated with normal right living. Painful but willing asceticism, in order to obtain mastery of the body and animal soul, and so free the will and soul from sense slavery, may be necessary in some in whom the appetites, passion, and desires have got the upper hand; but the life of an ascetic or a yogi who has mastered both Hatha and Raja Yoga is not a vocation adaptable or necessary to all, although attainable under natural law.

No word helps the student to understand his place in the universe more than the word "growth." If the universe is made for man and not man for the universe, then its dominant daily and important lesson is growth, and not pleasure only. Growth is as indefinite as progress unless the end is known, and that is why it is stated, but not dogmatically, that, so far as can be penetrated, the universe exists for soul unfoldment. This is the declaration of ancient and modern revelation, and the ultimate purpose of evolution. Both Theosophy and Spiritualism make it the supreme object of creation.

If this is so, then the unfoldment of the soul should be the theme of education, vocational work, life itself, and all minor and less important ends should be subsidiary to it. Service, not self-aggrandizement, doing good and not the pursuit of pleasure, nobility of character, purity of life, moral and intellectual culture, scientific attainments, should be sought. These spiritual possessions should weigh heavily against mere fame, position, and wealth. And while among the few there is still an innate love of and respect for this higher life and ideal, and a reverent appreciation of anyone who chooses and lives it, the vulgar fawning to the moneyed class is an outgrowth of the commercial spirit which is blighting the efforts of the scholar, the preacher, the educator, the humanitarian. and the old-school lover of simple living, and making the future very doubtful and precarious. Against the spiritual uplift and care of the youth overwhelming odds of reasonably sound moral and intellectual training of our boys and girls in schools and homes are the enormous counter-suggestiveness, cheap talk, slang, sensational and vulgar newspaper claptrap, and deadly home-destroying tendencies of the stage, society, the dance-hall. And many sane husbands and wives are deliberately choosing race-suicide to the assumption of the responsibility of a child under such sinister and home-wrecking conditions. Of course, this flighty, superficial, flippant, immoral state of the age is a transient phenomenon, due as much to the breaking down of the old moral standards as to the theological ideals of life which have governed the homes for generations; and yet the worst insidious effect of materialism is not in religion or irreligion, belief or unbelief, but in life. The Christian Church has yielded as much to this temptation as the children of the world. The swing of the pendulum of materialism has dipped, however, pretty nearly as deep into the mire as it is possible, and unquestionably the rebound will find men and women sick unto death of the injustice, poverty, disease, selfishness, immorality, insanity, idiocy, degeneracy, crime, and general rottenness into which our present boasted physical civilization and its consequent material living, each one for himself, at any cost or sacrifice, has plunged us. The remedy is not far to seek. The disease offers so many complex symptoms which are difficult to get at. Still, the law as well as purpose of the universe is not mocked. The impressiveness of the sovereignty of Divinity is perceived and realized in this fact. Modern revelation through the teachings of the spirit people brings home to us all the great fact that neither pain nor sorrow, disease nor death, are unrelated effects or are due to a malevolent purpose in the universe. They are not punitive but remedial, and while severe, they are never cruel nor vindictive. In fact, it is clearly shown in hypnosis that pain is sensational, and can be destroyed by thought. Thought can produce and destroy pain, for it is a builder or destroyer; and because this is so, nature's causality sits enthroned in a man's will, the highest expression of his Divinity. The old Egyptian aphorism, "As it is above, so is it below; as it is within, so is it without," applies to the use we make of thought. The body, created of cells, is the product of our thoughts in a way which neither the physicist, chemist, nor psychologist has made clear; and yet these cells respond to negative and positive thought in a way to invite disease or health, life or death. This discovery of the New Psychology gives a scientific rather than a supernatural interpretation to the alleged miracles of Jesus. And since this power to build or destroy our bodies and minds resides in ourselves, and is not the obsession of an outside malevolent power in the universe, nor wholly that of evil or undeveloped spirits, we learn that our worst enemy or our best friend is ourselves. Thus the universe conspires to exalt the soul that serves its Divinity!

The survival of the fit is more a spiritual than a physical triumph. The superman, unless it stands for humanity *minus* brute or dynamic force or violence, is doomed to defeat. This is hinted by the historical allegory of Goliath and David, and made manifest in every war which sweeps the earth. This is also why, as Matthew Arnold once said in his lecture on "Numbers," "majorities are usually wrong." The average intelligence may furnish a moral critique for or dictate the code or standards of morals of the people, but it is the supernormal man who knows what is best. So the supernormal man is the utilitarian genius of the future, as well as the ideal leader of the present age. Man supernormalized stands head and shoulders above the normal and average man. Nature qualifies him with intelligence as luminous as the sun. He stands on the apex of present human achievement and soul unfoldment and scans the infinitude of space like a god, and, conjuring with darkness, be brings forth out of seeming vacuity the dawn of a greater and happier age. Others, yes, the majority, go down to death for his sake, because he is the long-promised type of the superphysical (spiritual) man, born out of the travail of the past ages. He becomes the prophecy of unborn generations.

Forms, organs, personalities, are atrophied or discarded, when they impede progress and block soul unfoldment. Slowly but surely nature achieves her ends. The morning star shines for all eyes, but those who sleep know not of the morning. The vision appears only in souls who have qualified themselves to be conscious of its shimmering but far-distant presence.

The next step in human evolution is the genius of the sixth sense, the fourth dimensional man, the divine Adam, who can tell us that these spiritual realities and revelations which the lay mind can only accept through physical tests or on the authority of those who know are the visions and voices of the God in us all, that, though dormant, yet are manifest in others who having eyes see and ears hear the unutterable things of the spirit. The universe lifts him up to be the guide and guardian of the holy grail. Blood is sacrificed for grey matter of the brain, the brain for life, life for intelligence, intelligence for light, light for truth. Yet in losing light and gaining truth, man becomes not less human or virile, but more himself, more divine than ever. This is the logos (law) incarnate—EMANUEL, "God with us," the theme of the universe, hidden in biology, and at last revealed in the New Psychology which shows man the process by whch the soul ascends to its sovereignty of Divinity.

Three results or endowments of spiritual evolution or soul unfoldment stand preeminently forth as worthy of consideration.

Especially is this so because, when the spiritual and physical hemispheres of the universe are analogically compared (so far as comparison is possible), the causality of both worlds being spirit, show connected design and not chance, so far as these results are concerned. These results are physical and psychic sensitiveness, consciousness, and spirituality. The one has to do with the nervo-psychic body, and proves one a sensitive, keyed to the finest vibrations; the next has to do with the supernormal faculties which have been awakened and quickened; and the last has to do with one's character or life, and shows a spirit of broadest toleration, patience, and unselfishness.

The first result is, in a sense, dependent upon the last; and while some are born with it, it is susceptible of unfoldment as is any other endowment. Sympathy for others, benevolence, pity, kindness, unselfishness in every form of service, spiritualize as it ennobles one's nature, at the same time sensitizing the nervous system so that it becomes responsive to auras and magnetic influences. It is this sensitiveness which differentiates a fine, receptive from a coarse, obtuse organism. The finer the body, the more etherealized it is, and, as a result, the more sensitive. This kinesthesia is a new sensitiveness, not usual or common, except among highly strung and nervous people. Certain persons, called mediums, are such sensitives because of this organic susceptibility. It is dangerous when not understood or controlled, because, psychologically speaking, these sensitives feel and often impersonate each one's physical and mental condition, and therefore the need of knowledge and training to hold it in leash and throw off, or fortify oneself against these outside influences.

A great deal has been written against the

psychological crime of yielding to outside excarnate or incarnate influences, because of obsessions of a most dangerous sort. There is as grave danger from auto-suggestion and hypnosis, which may subjectively submerge the ego into a subconscious or abnormal state of mind which may end in some form of insanity. The reader needs only to be reminded that, while cases exist, they are rare, when the total population is considered. Worry, fear, drink, maternity, religious excitement, overwork, are the common sources of insanity. However, if as Vivekananda and other teachers of occult science advise, the student lives a reasonably rational, spiritual life, there is nothing to fear. Obsession by domination is, as a rule and in practice, among weak or feeble-minded men and women, and not among the strong, physically, mentally, and spiritually. Somnambules and mediums are a class by themselves. To feel outside influences is not necessarily a sign of obsession. If this were so, then the man or woman who feels anything would be more or less obsessed, which, in the strict use of the word, is absurd. To be obsessed, in an occult sense, is to be possessed or dominated by spirit influences or a hypnotist. And few indeed are or care to be so obsessed. The training required to maintain one's equilibrium through equanimity is to be able not only to separate our own impulses and impressions, however subtile and hidden, from similar impulses and impressions which by telepathy or sensitiveness we derive from without, but to form no sense habits by negotiating pleasing sensations at the risk of losing one's self-control or possession. Self-possession and not obsession follows the sane, spiritual use one makes of all experience, from whatever source. The incubus of any domination not self-elected or invited by harbouring one's physical sense pleasures is at a minimum, and becomes impossible in due course of time. Because as the soul unfolds, the higher self rises to sovereignty, and controls or displaces the lower ; and so, while one becomes a vicar, as did Jesus, for the psychological effects of other soul's physical and mental conditions, he, as master, knows how to interpret them, profit by them, and rise above them. As a rule, psychic sensitiveness is not so physically or organically acute as mediumistic susceptibility, and therefore the higher the life and finer the thought, the less liable is the psychic, at least, to take on other soul's conditions. This is a wise inhibition, for it affords the spiritually awakened the means to receive the mental impression of a condition without suffering the physical effect or vicarious pain. The universe thus conspires to help the soul that is ready to lay the foundation for the attainment of spiritual knowledge, communion, revelations, and understanding not afforded the gross, materially minded men and women who, allegorically, resemble the five foolish virgins. To such no ordeal, suffering, or sacrifice is without its important lesson and vision of triumphant and final victory and happiness.

The second result is consciousness—not sensation, thought, or the perception of sensation and thought, but consciousness as the attribute of Divinity, which, as it is realized, makes one aware of the eternal self—that self which is never born and therefore never dies. This fact is the supreme revelation of the New Psychology, as it has to do with our supernormal faculties and life. For when once this consciousness is realized, it, like a searchlight, can be used to illumine the hitherto occult and mysterious connections between our spiritual and physical functions, faculties, and being. Strange as this seems, it is stranger indeed that man did not follow his thought to consciousness and consciousness of the thought to his self-consciousness, but perceived only the outward, physical forms and sources of sensation. If Spiritualism (not Spiritism, which has most to do with proofs of the survival of the personality of death and of spirit communications) means and reveals anything, it is, that the consciousness is *a priori*—that is, it is of Divinity. Perception is not consciousness, nor self-consciousness, because it is not awareness. The realization or awareness of one's Divinity is the great revelation of nature's plan. Whoever receives it may be congratulated, as it is the step out of darkness to light. Consciousness is concerned with illumination. It is the illuminator and enlightener of the soul. The ego makes progress and unfoldment by and through it. It may inspire thought, without revealing its supreme function, to make each soul or ego aware of its own Divinity. In each sense, perception and thought, however objective, the consciousness is employed. Unconsciousness is merely its organic and functional inhibition, not its loss or destruction. Consciousness is not a substance, but a state, and as such it exists independent of organ or brain, thought or mind—is, in fact, uncreate and eternal. And here is the important fact which its knowledge affords, that once anyone is convinced of its reality and eternality, death has lost its terror and life has received its supreme sovereignty. For then, whatever one's extremity, whether it be poverty or pain, persecution or martyrdom, calumny or dishonour, the fadeless star of everlasting light has risen in his soul, to illumine the way to paradise. Think of what consciousness means, not only on the lower planes of sense and perception, but on the higher planes of supernormal faculties. Owing to our nervo-psychic organism, pleasures and pains alternate with unbalanced regularity; but in the consciousness, lifted above sense perception and concentrated on the formless self, as the vision of one's Divinity, that which survives death is the personality *plus*, but not less one's individual identity which feels no pain nor pleasure, but thus resurrected becomes, as it were, the adept or master, and in the third degree of development, putting on the yellow robe of the golden light of his Divinity, truly declaring at his own tomb—the body—" Even though he were dead, yet shall he live." And this too before death, while yet in the midst of dying. Consciousness thus brings to us this higher vision which only those who ascend the mountain of self-consciousness will enjoy. And added to this is the quickening of the " spiritual gifts, " the supernormal powers, which made it possible for Jesus to see the angel in the Garden of Gethsemane, and all to enjoy equally helpful, comforting, spiritual, and angelic ministrations.

And, finally, the one quality of life, spirituality, let none forget, for if it be true at last in theory and practice that the "meek shall inherit the earth" and the battle is not to the physically strong, the superman, and, indeed, all who expect to realize and enjoy life to its fullest expression, must possess this quality.

Spirituality is the opposite of materiality. It is the truest test of discipleship, service, and spiritual unfoldment, for any outward, formal profession of moral doctrine, or even any initiation into an occult Order, valuable as any such knowledge is from an intellectual standpoint, is valueless unless one lives the life. Of course, the public is not the judge, but one's conscience, and therefore grave danger from Pharisaism might follow an arbitrary court of judgment whose office is to measure the nice balance which exists between what we are and what the public think we are. So God and conscience must be the daily tribunal or judge.

Spirituality sublimes and purifies the life, and the nominal religionist, be he Brahmin, Taoist, Shintoist, Vishnuite, Sivaite, Buddhist,

Jew, Christian, or Mohammedan, is not a true disciple of his God or Master if, failing to live the spritual life, he professes only the creed and is a member only of the sect. This is the quality of the life which measured the value of the widow's mite above the outward perfunctory gifts or services of the Levite, and which truly advances one in the universal kingdom of spiritually illumined and beatified souls. This quality of spirituality is life's levitator and levitation. For it and it alone qualifies life as higher, as materiality qualifies it as lower. The higher one's life, the greater and purer the degree of spirituality.

Need it be said that spirituality gives reliability, truthfulness, and divine regard or love to a soul's sphere of service, and that one's Divinity expresses itself more and more fully through it than through merely the intellectual or mechanical use of psychical or supernormal powers?

This is important to remember, because the perception and intuition of truth is not so much a merely mathematical calculation, but a law of one's spiritual vision, dependent on one's spirituality.

Too much has been made of mediumship, spirit control, spirit communication, even development of psychical and supernormal powers, from a technical standpoint alone, and not enough of spirituality, since all true spiritual unfoldment rests upon it. Spirituality is the keystone of religion, the cornerstone of seership, the foundation of character and individuality, and the most helpful source of divine knowledge and understanding. It melts away the mists which obscure the mind to visions and voices celestial. It, more than any other quality of the spirit, except the will, makes possible self-control and self-mastery, and rivets the chain of the common daily facts of life with eternal compensations. Without it, eyes look across the abyss of time and see only darkness; but with it, time is bridged by a ladder of light, on which angels wait to welcome the pilgrim. Without it, the soul is like a cañon, fearful and terrorizing in its chasms of unexplored mysteries; but with it, the trail is seen which leads from darkness to light. Spirituality is the word whispered to the one who first used it by an angel, because it is celestial and not terrestrial in its origin. And because it furnishes the key which unlocks the book of life, revealing spiritual mysteries, it is a fact that no other word in the English language is so auxiliary of revelations. Let its magic staff touch the eyes, and they instantly become clairvoyant; the ears, and they become clairaudient;

the affections, and they become clairsentient; the mind, and it becomes inspired; the consciousness, and it becomes illuminated. It brings the light that never was on sea or land —the puissant, ineffable light of the spirit. It alone furnishes the passport to God. It is the symbolic lighted candle which Simon placed on the table as the light of the Gentile world, the Alpha and Omega of human apotheosis.

And when the earth, aye, the universe, is rolled up as a scroll and vanishes into nothingness, the psychic records which will live in heaven when all others are for ever forgotten will be those written in the fadeless light of our spirituality. If the universe, circumstancing unity of law and life, condenses all her wealth of power, knowledge, love, happiness in any three gifts of God to man, they are this trinity, sensitiveness, consciousness, and spirituality, without which one's Divinity, immortality, and happiness could not be assured on this or the other side of the grave. Whatever other eschatological summary and teleological purpose the universe may have in her creation, the means to man's perfection must ever be held in reverent esteem, for there can be no higher aim and purpose in any other theme or scheme of life than the soul's apotheosis and happiness.